T0145174

On the Other Side

Isabella Macdonald Smith

with

Sophia O. Smith, R.N.

This book is a work of non-fiction. Unless otherwise noted, the author and the publisher make no explicit guarantees as to the accuracy of the information contained in this book and in some cases, names of people and places have been altered to protect their privacy.

AuthorHouse™
1663 Liberty Drive
Bloomington, IN 47403
www.authorhouse.com
Phone: 833-262-8899

Because of the dynamic nature of the Internet, any web addresses or links contained in this book may have changed since publication and may no longer be valid. The views expressed in this work are solely those of the author and do not necessarily reflect the views of the publisher, and the publisher hereby disclaims any responsibility for them.

Any people depicted in stock imagery provided by Getty Images are models, and such images are being used for illustrative purposes only.
Certain stock imagery © Getty Images.

This book is printed on acid-free paper.

ISBN: 978-1-6655-5865-5 (sc)
ISBN: 978-1-6655-5866-2 (hc)
ISBN: 978-1-6655-5867-9 (e)

Library of Congress Control Number: 2022908243

Print information available on the last page.

Published by AuthorHouse 05/19/2022

author HOUSE®

FEATURED ON THE FRONT COVER

Cover Concept   **Annabella Rossi, LEED GA**
Interior Designer
Asheville, North Carolina

Front and Back
Cover Illustrator   **Melissa Margaret George, Student of Architecture,**
Class of 2024
Louisiana State University, Baton Rouge, Louisiana

Cover Depiction   **Perched on Tree Branches**
Oden's Two Ravens Observe

Spirits From the Other Side
Caliphur Blues Smith, Himalayan-Siamese
And Brittany Ann Smith, Border Collie

Watching Over
Lakota Smith, Siberian Husky

Back Cover   **Butterfly in Memory of Barbara Willard**
Haller Ballet, Covington, Louisiana

On the Other Side

Isabella MacDonald Smith
December 2020

Eulogy Author
Sophia O. Smith, RN

Ode to Caliphur Blues Smith
Himalayan-Siamese
Passing
Surrounded by Family

November 30, 2020
3:30 p.m.

////

Photo of Sophia and her father,
Frank Knowles Smith III

Upon a day
In the year 1998,
When

I was four years old,
I asked Dad if I could have a cat.

Dad read about you in the newspaper
Your name was Leon, and you weren't friendly.

I wanted to name you Blue's Clues,
But Dad and Mama KK said no.

Caliphur Blues Smith
Is the name I chose.

3

For over twenty-two years,

You gave me sass.
You were always trying to run away.
You gave me random dead animals.
You stole my stocks.
You scratched me.
You gave me love.

You wanted canned savory salmon at
three o'clock in the morning.

I miss our naps on the couch.
I miss being the only person you'd let

Hold
And
Hug
You.

I miss you standing in the shower, howling.
You wanted to drink the shower water.
I miss your sandpaper tongue
Licking my eyelids.

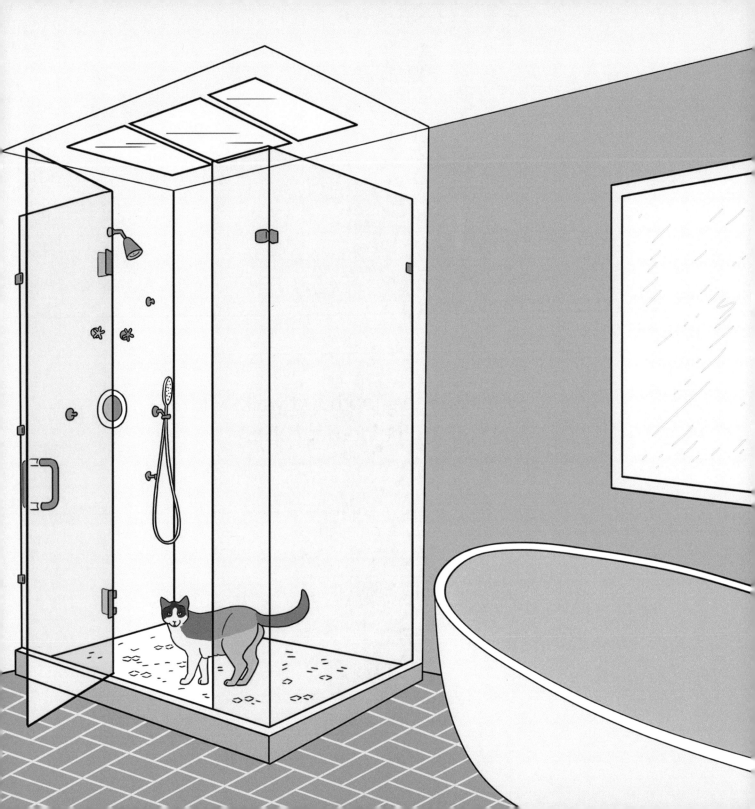

I miss our neighborhood walks with
Britt, the border collie.

You taught Lakota, the Siberian husky, how to howl.

Jolynn keeping watch over Caliphur.

You were the best cat sibling.
I am sad that I cannot give you
One more squeeze.

Thank you for giving us the best
Twenty-two years of your life.

Sophia cried
the day Caliphur passed.

Cast of Characters:

Brittany

Caliphur

Lakota

Sophia

Brittany

Caliphur and Sophia

Lakota and Sophia

Printed in the United States
by Baker & Taylor Publisher Services